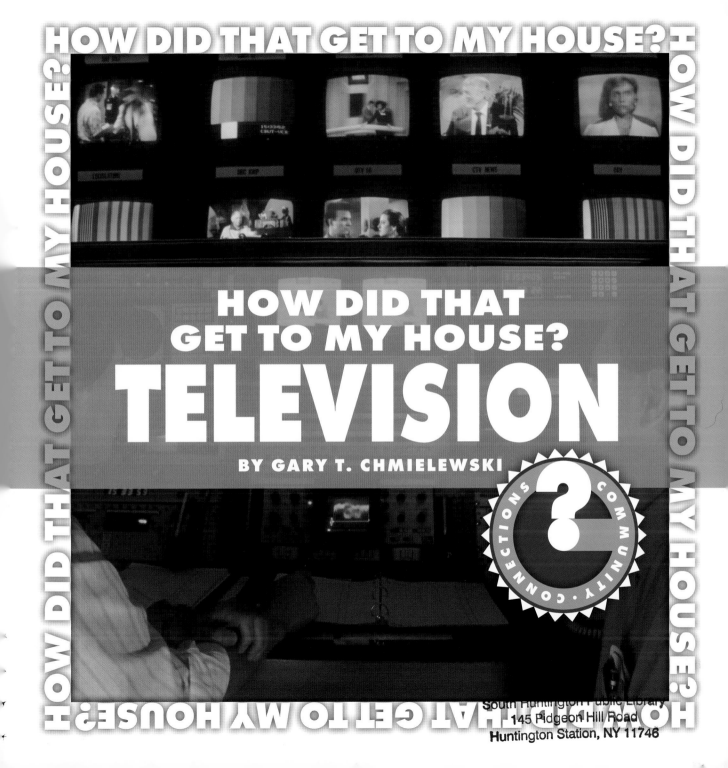

HOW DID THAT GET TO MY HOUSE?
TELEVISION

BY GARY T. CHMIELEWSKI

COMMUNITY · CONNECTIONS

CHERRY
LAKE
Publishing

TELEVISION

Published in the United States of America by Cherry Lake Publishing
Ann Arbor, Michigan
www.cherrylakepublishing.com

Content Adviser: Mary Raber, Associate Director, Institute for Interdisciplinary
Studies, Michigan Technological University
Reading Adviser: Cecilia Minden-Cupp, PhD, Literacy Consultant

Photo Credits: Cover and page 1, ©Lloyd Sutton/Alamy; page 5, ©DeshaCAM, used under
license from Shutterstock, Inc.; page 7, ©iStock.com/DeannaBean; page 9, ©Lagui, used under
license from Shutterstock, Inc.; page 11, ©Igorsky, used under license from Shutterstock, Inc.;
page 13, ©Art Directors - Archive/Alamy; page 15, ©iStock.com/KLH49; page 17, ©foto.fritz,
used under license from Shutterstock, Inc.; page 19, ©Armonn/Dreamstime.com; page 21,
©Rob Marmion, used under license from Shutterstock, Inc.

LIBRARY OF CONGRESS CATALOGING-IN-PUBLICATION DATA
Chmielewski, Gary T.
  How did that get to my house? Television / by Gary T. Chmielewski.
     p. cm.—(Community connections)
  Includes bibliographical references and index.
  ISBN-13: 978-1-60279-476-4
  ISBN-10: 1-60279-476-6
  1. Television—Juvenile literature. I. Title. II. Title: Television. III.
Series.
  TK6640.C525 2009
  621.388—dc22   2009001197

Cherry Lake Publishing would like to acknowledge the
work of The Partnership for 21st Century Skills. Please
visit www.21stcenturyskills.org for more information.

CONTENTS

HOW DID THAT GET TO MY HOUSE?

WHAT MAKES TELEVISION WORK?

Have you ever wondered how TV shows get to the screen? **Television stations** use special cameras. The cameras turn the pictures they record into **signals**. A TV set turns the signals back into shows you can watch.

Television shows are often recorded at a TV station.

TV signals come into your house in several ways. One way is called **broadcast TV**. Another way is **cable** TV. Finally, there is **satellite** TV. Each way is very different. People can choose which way they like best.

Do you like watching TV with your family?

How do you receive
TV signals at your
house? If you don't
know, ask an adult.
Ask your friends
how they receive
TV signals. Is it the
same way you
receive them?

TV SIGNALS

TV stations send signals using very tall towers. The signals travel through the air. You cannot see them, though. You can't touch them, either. An **antenna** is needed to receive TV signals. This type of TV is called broadcast TV. Anyone with an antenna can watch broadcast television for free.

You can see TV towers, but you can't see the signals that they send out.

9

TV signals travel from the antenna to the TV through a wire. The TV turns the signals into pictures and sound. Some older TVs need special equipment to help them do this. Then you can watch your favorite show. Can you believe that TV shows float through the air?

You may need an antenna on top of your house to watch broadcast TV.

Can you think of other things that use signals from the air? Think of things that have antennas. Hint: How do you phone a friend or listen to music?

Many people don't use broadcast TV anymore. They use cable or satellite TV. These types of TV cost money to use. Cable and satellite TV have many more channels than broadcast TV. That means there are more shows to choose from. These types of TV get to your house differently than broadcast TV.

You need to attach a special cable box to your TV to watch cable channels.

13

Cable companies collect signals from TV stations. Then they put them into one signal. This signal is sent out over a series of cables. These cables come into your house. They connect with your TV. The cable company charges you for using their signals.

You need a special cord to connect your TV to a cable box.

Satellite TV companies combine signals from many stations. They send the signals to a satellite above Earth. The signals bounce off the satellite and return to Earth. **Satellite dishes** are attached to houses. They pick up the signals. The dishes use wires to send the signals to TVs.

Satellite dishes are often attached to the roof of a house.

NO TV SET NEEDED

Today, you can watch TV shows on cell phones or iPods. You can watch TV shows almost anytime you want. You don't even have to be at home!

Many people like to watch TV shows while they are away from home.

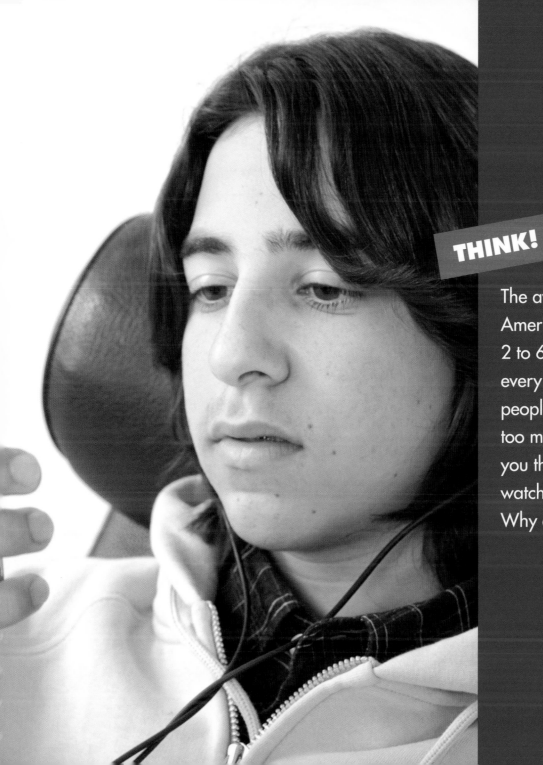

The average American watches 2 to 6 hours of TV every day. Many people say that is too much TV. Do you think it is bad to watch a lot of TV? Why or why not?

19

You can also watch TV on your home computer. You only need an **Internet** connection. Many TV networks let you watch their shows online. All you have to do is visit their Web sites.

Have you ever heard of YouTube.com? This Web site lets people make their own online TV shows. Anyone can watch them online. The possibilities for new shows are endless!

Have you ever watched a TV show on a computer?

21

GLOSSARY

antenna (an-TEN-uh) a wire that receives TV signals

broadcast TV (BRAWD-kast TEE-VEE) television that is received through signals in the air

cable (KAY-buhl) a bundle of wires that carry signals for television and other forms of communication

Internet (IN-tur-net) the electronic network that allows computers around the world to connect and share information

satellite (SAT-uh-lite) a spacecraft that orbits Earth and helps transmit TV signals and other forms of communication

satellite dishes (SAT-uh-lite DISH-ez) receivers that pick up TV signals and are attached to the walls or roofs of buildings

signals (SIG-nuhlz) electrical pulses sent out to carry TV shows or other forms of communication

television stations (TEL-uh-vizh-uhn STAY-shunz) places where a TV channel's signal is sent from

FIND OUT MORE

BOOKS

Bodden, Valerie. *Television*. Mankato, MN: Creative Education, 2008.

Raum, Elizabeth. *The History of the Television*. Chicago: Heinemann Library, 2008.

WEB SITES

FCC Kids Zone—The History of . . . Satellite TV Systems
www.fcc.gov/cgb/kidszone/history_sat_tv.html
Learn more about how satellite TV was invented

HowItWorks.net—How Television Works: Lights, Camera, Action!
www.howitworks.net/how-television-tv-works.html
Find out more about how a television set turns TV signals into shows you can watch

INDEX

ABOUT THE AUTHOR

Gary Chmielewski is a former library director. His career in children's publishing for the school and library market ranges from purchasing director of a major book wholesaler to executive for a prestigious children's and young adult publisher.

16(2)

95-64